YOUTH WRITER'S CAMP

youthwriterscamp.com

in partnership with
Youth Enterprise, Inc.

GREETINGS TO ALL!

Welcome to those who have decided to give this young author's first book a read. We believe in youth and their stories so much that we believed we could be a part of helping them to tell them and change them.

Our Youth Writers Camp provides continuous opportunities for healthy emotional expression within a safe and supportive community. Our goal is to not only help young people cope through writing, but also to motivate them to develop their own streams of revenue.

When Thunder Speaks, LLC is actively engaging today's youth with an aim to increase mental and emotional health outcomes. However, we understand that our efforts to positively impact the mental and emotional health of this current generation won't reach maximum effectiveness unless we have the support of the entire community. *THIS IS WHERE YOU COME IN.*

Through the things they discovered about themselves, the lessons about mental health, and the coping techniques they garnered during this time, it is our job as a community to continue to cultivate it and empower them to shift their own realities into the best versions designed for them. Our hope is that these students feel loved, cared for, and equipped enough to continue to heal and process with healthy coping tools and creative avenues. Thank you for investing into this student, one poem at a time.

Brandon Allen, Founder of When Thunder Speaks, LLC

THE
STORM
INSIDE

THE STORM INSIDE

MICAH AMOS

MAMA'S KITCHEN PRESS

The Storm Inside
©2021 Micah Amos
ISBN: 979-8-9853373-2-7

First Edition, 2021

Printed in the United States of America

Cover & Layout Design by Emily Anne Evans

CONTENTS

THE
STORM
INSIDE

GOALS

Goals are like football.

The ball can fly high,

easily be intercepted by others.

Goals are the main things that drive us to expectation.

But can break up the minute nothing goes your way.

I don't know how they make other people feel.

I'm going to tell you this:

If you have a goal, keep it.

If you work hard you will get there.

FEARS

Used to be self conscious but I learned that to be happy with

the way I am

I improve off of others judgement

It's was a great way to improve

I'm not focusing on the bad of the comments

but as a way to improve my mental and psychical state

I didn't accept my faith and made a change so I can prove them all

wrong

LIFE

Life is a tree ready to grow

the more you come together your roots will
grow

and some leaves may fall off at a matter of time

but it's never a goodbye

in do time the friendship will survive

the roots are a foundation for a tree to grow

over time it will show

it represents the bonds of the people we know

DEATH

Death is something that I fear

but always comes near

It's something we all have to face

but it ends in a tragedy

Death always greets with his for formalities

For time is like an hourglass

for when there's no more

It's his time to shine

quicker than an old person

wanting a quarter or dime.

MY JOURNEY

A journey can last a day of a year or more but it's up to you

Venture out for more.

If your journey consist of doing great things

make sure you write them down

so you won't lose insight of those things

Make sure you list all your hopes and when you reach them check them off

It will cost time and money but will be worth it

when you can sit back and say

I desire all of this.

WILLPOWER

Willpower will keep you down

it will lead to things that might depress you and
feel more low and down

You have to grab your willpower and fight

to expose all the bad habits and be determined
to keep up the fight.

Fight for everything you need and want

you have the willpower to see if it comes about.

Willpower to stand and never fall again

Willpower to say i'm going to try again

Willpower to do something new

Willpower to make forward

Willpower to show myself that I am important

When I make it then I will say

I have willpower help me to be this way

say have willpower help me to be this way.

MENTAL HEALTH

Struggles about living with good mental health
is a challenge

I felt like being a cage trapped from the outside
world

I'm glad I go to highschool but it makes me

Feel like we'll never live the same again

People can't go outside without having a fear
of dying

People can't socialize without wearing mask

It's making people mad people protesting for
their right

but is it worth it in the end?

OVERCOME

No matter the problem time of day

I stay positive to overcome the things that I go through

Overcome Negativity, doubt and fears.

Telling myself I am strong and block all my fears.

Knowing all things are possible and I truly believe I'm going to make it

The top with thinking of my fears

That I can do all things in Christ with strength.

CONFIDENT

When I stick with something I am confident about it

No changing my mind and people saying no not for you

I put my mind to it.

I am me and no one else can see my heart, my mind and goals.

So confident I will achieve my goals, maybe not today or tomorrow

but someday I will.

TRANSPARENT

My life feels transparent

One day it's full of color

Then the next day its dull full of white and empty thoughts

But my dreams are not transparent

they are the thing that drives me to become a better person

have meaning so I may feel transparent

but it will always go back to a full ray of colors

don't give up because there are dull or transparent days

because there are more days when you're going to enjoy life

find the positives

ABOUT THE AUTHOR

My name is Micah Amos. I was born in Illinois and am 14 years old. I love to learn, and family and friends are very important to me.

www.ingramcontent.com/pod-product-compliance
Lightning Source LLC
Chambersburg PA
CBHW072057040426
42447CB00012BB/3160